Stefan Abresch
Life Songs of Adv

Life Songs of Advent

Scripture Reflections for the Christmas Season

By:

Stefan G. Abresch

Pastor Ernestine,

Thank you for the hospitality and love of your family and friends today. You are an anointing of Christ upon us. May the grace and joy of this seasons remain with you always. Great love to you and your community.

In Christ,

Stefan Abresch

Stefan Abresch
Life Songs of Advent

Acknowledgements

This book is dedicated to my Parents who have supported all my efforts, my family who has always been there for me, my friends for their prayers, support, and the love of God that I have learned through their witness, to my Editor, Kathy who took the time to help make this book what God's wants it to be, and to Demetria who has strengthened, encouraged, loved me, and challenged me to always reach for the higher things which come from God.

Stefan Abresch
Life Songs of Advent

All people referred in this book are friends who I have met on my journey who have made an impact in my life. Any reference to any other people living or dead is purely coincidental.

All scriptures were retrieved from the United States Conference of Catholic Bishops website: http://www.usccb.org/bible/readings

ISBN-13: 978-1493680252

1st Sunday of Advent

1st Reading Is 2:1-5
This is what Isaiah, son of Amoz,
saw concerning Judah and Jerusalem.
In days to come,
the mountain of the LORD's house
shall be established as the highest mountain
and raised above the hills.
All nations shall stream toward it;
many peoples shall come and say:
"Come, let us climb the LORD's mountain,
to the house of the God of Jacob,
that he may instruct us in his ways,
and we may walk in his paths."
For from Zion shall go forth instruction,
and the word of the LORD from Jerusalem.
He shall judge between the nations,
and impose terms on many peoples.
They shall beat their swords into plowshares
and their spears into pruning hooks;
one nation shall not raise the sword against another,
nor shall they train for war again.
O house of Jacob, come,
let us walk in the light of the Lord!

Psalm Ps 122:1-9
R. **Let us go rejoicing to the house of the Lord.**

I rejoiced because they said to me,
"We will go up to the house of the LORD."

And now we have set foot
within your gates, O Jerusalem.
R. **Let us go rejoicing to the house of the Lord.**

Jerusalem, built as a city
with compact unity.
To it the tribes go up,
the tribes of the LORD.
R. **Let us go rejoicing to the house of the Lord.**

According to the decree for Israel,
to give thanks to the name of the LORD.
In it are set up judgment seats,
seats for the house of David.
R. **Let us go rejoicing to the house of the Lord.**

Pray for the peace of Jerusalem!
May those who love you prosper!
May peace be within your walls,
prosperity in your buildings.
R. **Let us go rejoicing to the house of the Lord.**

Because of my brothers and friends
I will say, "Peace be within you!"
Because of the house of the LORD, our God,
I will pray for your good.
R. **Let us go rejoicing to the house of the Lord.**

2nd Reading Rom 13:11-14
Brothers and sisters:
You know the time;
it is the hour now for you to awake from sleep.
For our salvation is nearer now than when we first believed;
the night is advanced, the day is at hand.
Let us then throw off the works of darkness
and put on the armor of light;
let us conduct ourselves properly as in the day,
not in orgies and drunkenness,
not in promiscuity and lust,
not in rivalry and jealousy.
But put on the Lord Jesus Christ,
and make no provision for the desires of the flesh.

Gospel Mt 24:37-44
Jesus said to his disciples:
"As it was in the days of Noah,
so it will be at the coming of the Son of Man.
In those days before the flood,
they were eating and drinking,
marrying and giving in marriage,
up to the day that Noah entered the ark.
They did not know until the flood came and carried them all away.
So will it be also at the coming of the Son of Man.
Two men will be out in the field;
one will be taken, and one will be left.
Two women will be grinding at the mill;
one will be taken, and one will be left.

Therefore, stay awake!
For you do not know on which day your Lord will come.
Be sure of this:if the master of the house
had known the hour of night when the thief was coming,
he would have stayed awake
and not let his house be broken into.
So too, you also must be prepared,
for at an hour you do not expect, the Son of Man will come."

"The son of man will come." Mt 24:44

There was once a time when the Christmas Season was a time of loneliness for me. I focused more on the gift of someone special who I could share these precious moments with and overlooked someone special who was calling me to live in his moments. I had lost focused of the reason for the season which is Jesus Christ. I wanted something that I could touch while he was still reaching out in his own way to touch me. I had to learn to accept the gift and to realize that it was much greater than any gift or human relationship that I could ever receive.

There are many of us who are dealing with some sense of loneliness during this season. Some have lost a loved one and special friends this year. Some may live in different parts of the country away from their family and not have the means to join them. Some are serving our country in foreign lands. Loneliness does take a toll on people but God allows us to never be lonely. Somewhere in the world someone is praying for you. Someone in the world someone is longing to hold you. Somewhere in the world someone is thinking of you during this day. The Christ child was born to unite all people and through him, even though some may not be together during this season in person, the spirit of God has united us in faith, hope, and love.

1st Monday of Advent

1st Reading Is 4:2-6
On that day,
The branch of the LORD will be luster and glory,
and the fruit of the earth will be honor and splendor
for the survivors of Israel.
He who remains in Zion
and he who is left in Jerusalem
Will be called holy:
every one marked down for life in Jerusalem.
When the LORD washes away
the filth of the daughters of Zion,
And purges Jerusalem's blood from her midst
with a blast of searing judgment,
Then will the LORD create,
over the whole site of Mount Zion
and over her place of assembly,
A smoking cloud by day
and a light of flaming fire by night.
For over all, the LORD's glory will be shelter and protection:
shade from the parching heat of day,
refuge and cover from storm and rain.

Psalm Ps 122:1-9
R. **Let us go rejoicing to the house of the Lord.**

I rejoiced because they said to me,

“We will go up to the house of the LORD."
And now we have set foot
within your gates, O Jerusalem.
R. **Let us go rejoicing to the house of the Lord.**

Jerusalem, built as a city
with compact unity.
To it the tribes go up,
the tribes of the LORD.
R. **Let us go rejoicing to the house of the Lord.**

According to the decree for Israel,
to give thanks to the name of the LORD.
In it are set up judgment seats,
seats for the house of David.
R. **Let us go rejoicing to the house of the Lord.**

Pray for the peace of Jerusalem!
May those who love you prosper!
May peace be within your walls,
prosperity in your buildings.
R. **Let us go rejoicing to the house of the Lord.**

Because of my relatives and friends
I will say, “Peace be within you!"
Because of the house of the LORD, our God,
I will pray for your good.
R. **Let us go rejoicing to the house of the Lord.**

Gospel Mt 8:5-11
When Jesus entered Capernaum,
a centurion approached him and appealed to him, saying,
"Lord, my servant is lying at home paralyzed, suffering dreadfully."
He said to him, "I will come and cure him."
The centurion said in reply,
"Lord, I am not worthy to have you enter under my roof;
only say the word and my servant will be healed.
For I too am a man subject to authority,
with soldiers subject to me.
And I say to one, 'Go,' and he goes;
and to another, 'Come here,' and he comes;
and to my slave, 'Do this,' and he does it."
When Jesus heard this, he was amazed and said to those following him,
"Amen, I say to you, in no one in Israel have I found such faith.
I say to you, many will come from the east and the west,
and will recline with Abraham, Isaac, and Jacob
at the banquet in the Kingdom of heaven."

"Go." Mt 8:9

I have a friend named Greg and for many years we belonged to the same parish, served together in church ministries, studied scripture together, prayed together, and even saw each other once or twice a week while working. Then God placed a call on his heart, and Greg responded by going back to school, getting a master's degree in theology, and now is teaching.

The Centurion understood what it meant to "go." Mary, Joseph, Elizabeth, Zachariah, the three wise men, and all the people who played a part in the Christmas story understood it too. They each responded to the call to "go, " to do something or go somewhere in response to God's request, and they went because they trusted God. We also are called to "go" and do something for God. We go because we trust God. We go because we have come to know that with God all things work for good. We go because, in the end, we really do believe that the Christ child has been born to us as the Word made flesh. O come let us adore him.

1rst Tuesday of Advent

1st Reading Is. 11:1-10

On that day,
A shoot shall sprout from the stump of Jesse,
and from his roots a bud shall blossom.
The Spirit of the LORD shall rest upon him:
a Spirit of wisdom and of understanding,
A Spirit of counsel and of strength,
a Spirit of knowledge and of fear of the LORD,
and his delight shall be the fear of the LORD.
Not by appearance shall he judge,
nor by hearsay shall he decide,
But he shall judge the poor with justice,
and decide aright for the land's afflicted.
He shall strike the ruthless with the rod of his mouth,
and with the breath of his lips he shall slay the wicked.
Justice shall be the band around his waist,
and faithfulness a belt upon his hips.

Then the wolf shall be a guest of the lamb,
and the leopard shall lie down with the kid;
The calf and the young lion shall browse together,
with a little child to guide them.
The cow and the bear shall be neighbors,
together their young shall rest;
the lion shall eat hay like the ox.
The baby shall play by the cobra's den,
and the child lay his hand on the adder's lair.

There shall be no harm or ruin on all my holy mountain;
for the earth shall be filled with knowledge of the LORD,
as water covers the sea.

On that day,
The root of Jesse,
set up as a signal for the nations,
The Gentiles shall seek out,
for his dwelling shall be glorious.

Psalm Ps 72:1-2, 7-8, 12-13, 17
R. **Justice shall flourish in his time, and fullness of peace for ever.**

O God, with your judgment endow the king,
and with your justice, the king's son;
He shall govern your people with justice
and your afflicted ones with judgment.
R. **Justice shall flourish in his time, and fullness of peace for ever.**

Justice shall flower in his days,
and profound peace, till the moon be no more.
May he rule from sea to sea,
and from the River to the ends of the earth.
R. **Justice shall flourish in his time, and fullness of peace for ever.**

He shall rescue the poor when he cries out,
and the afflicted when he has no one to help him.

He shall have pity for the lowly and the poor;
the lives of the poor he shall save.
R. **Justice shall flourish in his time, and fullness of peace for ever.**

May his name be blessed forever;
as long as the sun his name shall remain.
In him shall all the tribes of the earth be blessed;
all the nations shall proclaim his happiness.
R. **Justice shall flourish in his time, and fullness of peace for ever.**

Gospel Lk 10:21-24
Jesus rejoiced in the Holy Spirit and said,
"I give you praise, Father, Lord of heaven and earth,
for although you have hidden these things
from the wise and the learned
you have revealed them to the childlike.
Yes, Father, such has been your gracious will.
All things have been handed over to me by my Father.
No one knows who the Son is except the Father,
and who the Father is except the Son
and anyone to whom the Son wishes to reveal him."

Turning to the disciples in private he said,
"Blessed are the eyes that see what you see.
For I say to you,
many prophets and kings desired to see what you see,

but did not see it,
and to hear what you hear, but did not hear it."

"Many Prophets and Kings desire to see what you see, but did not see it, and to hear what you hear and did not hear it." Lk 10:24

One morning I was on the roof at work and I saw the sunrise. I watched as the sun began to peak above the horizon and light up the eastern sky. It was a privilege to watch the world awake. An ordinary moment became extraordinary.

Mary lived an ordinary life until she was visited by the angel Gabriel. An ordinary moment became extraordinary for her, and it remains an extraordinary moment for us, too. In the angel's message, she heard words that prophets and kings longed to hear: that God is with us. Our Lord gave us the story of the nativity so that we can see and hear what our world is longing to know: that God is with us.

1st Wednesday of Advent

1st Reading Is 25:6-10
On this mountain the LORD of hosts
will provide for all peoples
A feast of rich food and choice wines,
juicy, rich food and pure, choice wines.
On this mountain he will destroy
the veil that veils all peoples,
The web that is woven over all nations;
he will destroy death forever.
The Lord GOD will wipe away
the tears from all faces;
The reproach of his people he will remove
from the whole earth; for the LORD has spoken.

On that day it will be said:
"Behold our God, to whom we looked to save us!
This is the LORD for whom we looked;
let us rejoice and be glad that he has saved us!"
For the hand of the LORD will rest on this mountain.

Psalm Ps 23:1-3A, 3B-4, 5, 6
R. **I shall live in the house of the Lord all the days of my life.**

The LORD is my shepherd; I shall not want.
In verdant pastures he gives me repose;
Beside restful waters he leads me;
he refreshes my soul.

R. **I shall live in the house of the Lord all the days of my life.**

He guides me in right paths
for his name's sake.
Even though I walk in the dark valley
I fear no evil; for you are at my side
With your rod and your staff
that give me courage.
R. **I shall live in the house of the Lord all the days of my life.**

You spread the table before me
in the sight of my foes;
You anoint my head with oil;
my cup overflows.
R. **I shall live in the house of the Lord all the days of my life.**

Only goodness and kindness follow me
all the days of my life;
And I shall dwell in the house of the LORD
for years to come.
R. **I shall live in the house of the Lord all the days of my life.**

Gospel Mt 15:29-37
At that time:
Jesus walked by the Sea of Galilee,
went up on the mountain, and sat down there.
Great crowds came to him,
having with them the lame, the blind, the deformed, the mute,

and many others.
They placed them at his feet, and he cured them.
The crowds were amazed when they saw the mute speaking,
the deformed made whole,
the lame walking,
and the blind able to see,
and they glorified the God of Israel.

Jesus summoned his disciples and said,
"My heart is moved with pity for the crowd,
for they have been with me now for three days and have nothing to eat.
I do not want to send them away hungry,
for fear they may collapse on the way."
The disciples said to him,
"Where could we ever get enough bread in this deserted place
to satisfy such a crowd?"
Jesus said to them, "How many loaves do you have?"
"Seven," they replied, "and a few fish."
He ordered the crowd to sit down on the ground.
Then he took the seven loaves and the fish,
gave thanks, broke the loaves,
and gave them to the disciples, who in turn gave them to the crowds.
They all ate and were satisfied.
They picked up the fragments left over–seven baskets full.

"They all ate and were satisfied. They picked up the fragments left over – seven baskets full." Mt 15:37

The Cursillo Movement is something that changed my life and continues to do so. It created a hunger for Christ within me; it made me a better person. The Cursillo community has gotten me through some of the darkest times of my life, and people in the movement have been a great blessing to me. You might say that Cursillo was the "basket," the way in which God conveyed the nourishment I needed to grow strong as a disciple of his Son.

God has many baskets and many ways of feeding us. He has an endless supply of blessings and can be very creative in how he bestows those blessings. What "baskets" has God used to bring blessings to you? Through what people, places and movements has God helped you grow as a disciple? In what way is God asking you to share your basket of blessings?

1st Thursday of Advent

1st Reading Is 26:1-6
On that day they will sing this song in the land of Judah:

"A strong city have we;
he sets up walls and ramparts to protect us.
Open up the gates
to let in a nation that is just,
one that keeps faith.
A nation of firm purpose you keep in peace;
in peace, for its trust in you."

Trust in the LORD forever!
For the LORD is an eternal Rock.
He humbles those in high places,
and the lofty city he brings down;
He tumbles it to the ground,
levels it with the dust.
It is trampled underfoot by the needy,
by the footsteps of the poor.

Psalm Ps 128:1, 8-9, 19-21, 25-27A
R. **Blessed is he who comes in the name of the Lord.**

Give thanks to the LORD, for he is good,
for his mercy endures forever.
It is better to take refuge in the LORD
than to trust in man.
It is better to take refuge in the LORD
than to trust in princes.

R. **Blessed is he who comes in the name of the Lord.**

Open to me the gates of justice;
I will enter them and give thanks to the LORD.
This gate is the LORD's;
the just shall enter it.
I will give thanks to you, for you have answered me
and have been my savior.
R. **Blessed is he who comes in the name of the Lord.**

O LORD, grant salvation!
O LORD, grant prosperity!
Blessed is he who comes in the name of the LORD;
we bless you from the house of the LORD.
The LORD is God, and he has given us light.
R. **Blessed is he who comes in the name of the Lord.**

Gospel Mt 7:21, 24-27
Jesus said to his disciples:
"Not everyone who says to me, 'Lord, Lord,'
will enter the Kingdom of heaven,
but only the one who does the will of my Father in heaven.

"Everyone who listens to these words of mine and acts on them
will be like a wise man who built his house on rock.

The rain fell, the floods came,
and the winds blew and buffeted the house.
But it did not collapse; it had been set solidly on rock.
And everyone who listens to these words of mine
but does not act on them
will be like a fool who built his house on sand.
The rain fell, the floods came,
and the winds blew and buffeted the house.
And it collapsed and was completely ruined."

"Everyone who listens to these words of mine and acts on them will be a wise man." Mt 7:24

I haven't always made the wisest decisions in my life. One bad decision was to enter into a marriage despite warning signs. The divorce left me broken, defeated, and without purpose. I would come home from work each day and just lock the door. Through it all God was working on a new beginning for me. Through him I found the healing, victory, and purpose I was looking for. My unwise actions eventually led to wisdom.

All of us have made bad decisions in our lives. God has the ability to restore us by his grace and make us stronger. We learn wisdom and become like the man who chose to build his house on the rock. Jesus is the Rock, and when we build our life on him, there is no storm that can tear us away.

1st Friday of Advent

1st Reading Is 29:17-24
Thus says the Lord GOD:
But a very little while,
and Lebanon shall be changed into an orchard,
and the orchard be regarded as a forest!
On that day the deaf shall hear
the words of a book;
And out of gloom and darkness,
the eyes of the blind shall see.
The lowly will ever find joy in the LORD,
and the poor rejoice in the Holy One of Israel.
For the tyrant will be no more
and the arrogant will have gone;
All who are alert to do evil will be cut off,
those whose mere word condemns a man,
Who ensnare his defender at the gate,
and leave the just man with an empty claim.
Therefore thus says the LORD,
the God of the house of Jacob,
who redeemed Abraham:
Now Jacob shall have nothing to be ashamed of,
nor shall his face grow pale.
When his children see
the work of my hands in his midst,
They shall keep my name holy;
they shall reverence the Holy One of Jacob,
and be in awe of the God of Israel.
Those who err in spirit shall acquire
understanding,
and those who find fault shall receive
instruction.

Psalm Ps 27:1, 4, 13-14
R. **The Lord is my light and my salvation.**

The LORD is my light and my salvation;
whom should I fear?
The LORD is my life's refuge;
of whom should I be afraid?
R. **The Lord is my light and my salvation.**

One thing I ask of the LORD;
this I seek:
To dwell in the house of the LORD
all the days of my life,
That I may gaze on the loveliness of the LORD
and contemplate his temple.
R. **The Lord is my light and my salvation.**

I believe that I shall see the bounty of the LORD
in the land of the living.
Wait for the LORD with courage;
be stouthearted, and wait for the LORD.
R. **The Lord is my light and my salvation.**

Gospel Mt 9:27-31
As Jesus passed by, two blind men followed
him, crying out,
"Son of David, have pity on us!"
When he entered the house,
the blind men approached him and Jesus said to
them,
"Do you believe that I can do this?"
"Yes, Lord," they said to him.

Then he touched their eyes and said,
"Let it be done for you according to your faith."
And their eyes were opened.
Jesus warned them sternly,
"See that no one knows about thIs"
But they went out and spread word of him
through all that land.

"Let it be done for you according to your faith." Mt 9:29

When my Father began the RCIA (Rite of Christian Initiation for Adults, the process for adults who want to become Catholic) at our home parish he realized it was something that he couldn't do alone. He asked many people to help, but few responded. One day in frustration he threw his hands up and said to God: "If you want this to work, you take care of it." And of course, God did.

Even when we are ministering to others, we want to be in control, to do things our way. We forget that God has a better plan, and to give him the control. We can work hard, or we can work smart, as the saying goes. Working with God and having faith that he will provide all we need to accomplish our tasks is the best way to strengthen our relationship with him.

1st Saturday of Advent

1st Reading Is 30:19-21, 23-26
Thus says the Lord GOD,
the Holy One of Israel:
O people of Zion, who dwell in Jerusalem,
no more will you weep;
He will be gracious to you when you cry out,
as soon as he hears he will answer you.
The Lord will give you the bread you need
and the water for which you thirst.
No longer will your Teacher hide himself,
but with your own eyes you shall see your Teacher,
While from behind, a voice shall sound in your ears:
"This is the way; walk in it,"
when you would turn to the right or to the left.

He will give rain for the seed
that you sow in the ground,
And the wheat that the soil produces
will be rich and abundant.
On that day your flock will be given pasture
and the lamb will graze in spacious meadows;
The oxen and the asses that till the ground
will eat silage tossed to them
with shovel and pitchfork.
Upon every high mountain and lofty hill
there will be streams of running water.
On the day of the great slaughter,
when the towers fall,
The light of the moon will be like that of the sun

and the light of the sun will be seven times greater
like the light of seven days.
On the day the LORD binds up the wounds of his people,
he will heal the bruises left by his blows.

Psalm Ps:147:1-2, 3-4, 5-6
R. **Blessed are all who wait for the Lord.**

Praise the LORD, for he is good;
sing praise to our God, for he is gracious;
it is fitting to praise him.
The LORD rebuilds Jerusalem;
the dispersed of Israel he gathers.
R. **Blessed are all who wait for the Lord.**

He heals the brokenhearted
and binds up their wounds.
He tells the number of the stars;
he calls each by name.
R. **Blessed are all who wait for the Lord.**

Great is our LORD and mighty in power:
to his wisdom there is no limit.
The LORD sustains the lowly;
the wicked he casts to the ground.
R. **Blessed are all who wait for the Lord.**

Gospel Mt 9:35-10:1, 5A, 6-8
Jesus went around to all the towns and villages,
teaching in their synagogues,
proclaiming the Gospel of the Kingdom,

and curing every disease and illness.
At the sight of the crowds, his heart was moved with pity for them
because they were troubled and abandoned,
like sheep without a shepherd.
Then he said to his disciples,
"The harvest is abundant but the laborers are few;
so ask the master of the harvest
to send out laborers for his harvest."

Then he summoned his Twelve disciples
and gave them authority over unclean spirits to drive them out
and to cure every disease and every illness.

Jesus sent out these Twelve after instructing them thus,
"Go to the lost sheep of the house of Israel.
As you go, make this proclamation:'The Kingdom of heaven is at hand.'
Cure the sick, raise the dead,
cleanse lepers, drive out demons.
Without cost you have received; without cost you are to give."

"Without cost you have received; without cost you are to give." Mt 10:8

I remember the first time I met one of my best friends, Charles. He showed up for a Cursillo weekend and didn't know what to expect. When he first introduced himself, I gave him a hug because I was happy to have him join us. He told me later that I was the first "stranger dude" ever to hug him. After the weekend I had the privilege of watching him grow in his relationship with Christ. He lives an inspired life and gives back more than he has received. He is an inspiration to many.

We are all called to live inspired lives. It requires us to be open and vulnerable which can be scary, but through the Holy Spirit we proclaim life through word and action. We cure the sick at heart; raise those who are in tombs of pain; we provide God's healing to the rejected and the outcast; we help drive out the demons of addiction, suffering, and sadness. We are the instruments that begin the work but it is God's hands the perfect the final masterpiece. We have been born to Christ and we witness to his birth in our lives so that he can be born in the lives of others.

2nd Sunday of Advent

1st reading Is 11:1-10
On that day, a shoot shall sprout from the stump of Jesse,
and from his roots a bud shall blossom.
The spirit of the LORD shall rest upon him:
a spirit of wisdom and of understanding,
a spirit of counsel and of strength,
a spirit of knowledge and of fear of the LORD,
and his delight shall be the fear of the LORD.
Not by appearance shall he judge,
nor by hearsay shall he decide,
but he shall judge the poor with justice,
and decide aright for the land's afflicted.
He shall strike the ruthless with the rod of his mouth,
and with the breath of his lips he shall slay the wicked.
Justice shall be the band around his waist,
and faithfulness a belt upon his hips
Then the wolf shall be a guest of the lamb,
and the leopard shall lie down with the kid;
the calf and the young lion shall browse together,
with a little child to guide them.
The cow and the bear shall be neighbors,
together their young shall rest;
the lion shall eat hay like the ox.
The baby shall play by the cobra's den,
and the child lay his hand on the adder's lair.
There shall be no harm or ruin on all my holy mountain;

for the earth shall be filled with knowledge of the LORD,
as water covers the sea.
On that day, the root of Jesse,
set up as a signal for the nations,
the Gentiles shall seek out,
for his dwelling shall be glorious.

Psalm Ps 72:1-2, 7-8, 12-13, 17
R. **Justice shall flourish in his time, and fullness of peace for ever.**

O God, with your judgment endow the king,
and with your justice, the king's son;
he shall govern your people with justice
and your afflicted ones with judgment.
R. **Justice shall flourish in his time, and fullness of peace for ever.**

Justice shall flower in his days,
and profound peace, till the moon be no more.
May he rule from sea to sea,
and from the River to the ends of the earth.
R. **Justice shall flourish in his time, and fullness of peace for ever.**

For he shall rescue the poor when he cries out,
and the afflicted when he has no one to help him.
He shall have pity for the lowly and the poor;
the lives of the poor he shall save.
R. **Justice shall flourish in his time, and fullness of peace for ever.**

May his name be blessed forever;
as long as the sun his name shall remain.
In him shall all the tribes of the earth be blessed;
all the nations shall proclaim his happiness.
R. **Justice shall flourish in his time, and fullness of peace for ever.**

2nd Reading Romans 15:4-9

Brothers and sisters:
Whatever was written previously was written for our instruction,
that by endurance and by the encouragement of the Scriptures
we might have hope.
May the God of endurance and encouragement
grant you to think in harmony with one another,
in keeping with Christ Jesus,
that with one accord you may with one voice
glorify the God and Father of our Lord Jesus Christ.

Welcome one another, then, as Christ welcomed you,
for the glory of God.
For I say that Christ became a minister of the circumcised
to show God's truthfulness,
to confirm the promises to the patriarchs,
but so that the Gentiles might glorify God for his mercy.
As it is written:

*Therefore, I will praise you among the Gentiles
and sing praises to your name.*

Gospel Mt 3:1-12

John the Baptist appeared, preaching in the desert of Judea
and saying, "Repent, for the kingdom of heaven is at hand!"
It was of him that the prophet Isaiah had spoken when he said:
*A voice of one crying out in the desert,
Prepare the way of the Lord,
make straight his paths.*
John wore clothing made of camel's hair
and had a leather belt around his waist.
His food was locusts and wild honey.
At that time Jerusalem, all Judea,
and the whole region around the Jordan
were going out to him
and were being baptized by him in the Jordan River
as they acknowledged their sins.

When he saw many of the Pharisees and Sadducees
coming to his baptism, he said to them, "You brood of vipers!
Who warned you to flee from the coming wrath?
Produce good fruit as evidence of your repentance.
And do not presume to say to yourselves,
'We have Abraham as our father.'

For I tell you,
God can raise up children to Abraham from these stones.
Even now the ax lies at the root of the trees.
Therefore every tree that does not bear good fruit
will be cut down and thrown into the fire.
I am baptizing you with water, for repentance,
but the one who is coming after me is mightier than I.
I am not worthy to carry his sandals.
He will baptize you with the Holy Spirit and fire.
His winnowing fan is in his hand.
He will clear his threshing floor
and gather his wheat into his barn,
but the chaff he will burn with unquenchable fire."

"Repent for the Kingdom of God is at hand." Mt 3:2

I am not someone who has always followed the straight and narrow. I have done many things that I am ashamed of. I thank God for his mercy because without it I would be heading non-stop on the down elevator. I have learned that because of God's mercy, along with sorrow for my sins, my record has been exonerated and the elevator has changed direction. I have been washed clean by a Love that is life-changing and healing. Forgiveness exists because of one person – Jesus – who was born so that all may be granted God's mercy.

Repentance leads to the restoration of our joy, a feeling of peace, and a deeper relationship with our God. Through mercy we are welcomed into God's grace and it changes us to make us better than we were before. We are prepared for the kingdom that has already come but is not yet fully here. Mercy is for anyone who is willing to accept it. When we accept the invitation of faith we become members of the kingdom of God, which is at hand. We are forgiven and restored to a life of grace so that during this Advent and Christmas season we may share Jesus, the light of the world. And now my life song sings.

2nd Monday of Advent (The Solemnity of the Immaculate Conception of Mary is transferred to Monday, Dec. 9 in 2013 because the Sunday readings take precedence on Dec. 8.)

1st Reading Gn 3:9-15, 20
After the man, Adam, had eaten of the tree,
the LORD God called to the man and asked him, "Where are you?"
He answered, "I heard you in the garden;
but I was afraid, because I was naked,
so I hid myself."
Then he asked, "Who told you that you were naked?
You have eaten, then,
from the tree of which I had forbidden you to eat!"
The man replied, "The woman whom you put here with me
she gave me fruit from the tree, and so I ate it."
The LORD God then asked the woman,
"Why did you do such a thing?"
The woman answered, "The serpent tricked me into it, so I ate it."

Then the LORD God said to the serpent:
"Because you have done this, you shall be banned
from all the animals
and from all the wild creatures;
on your belly shall you crawl,
and dirt shall you eat

all the days of your life.
I will put enmity between you and the woman,
and between your offspring and hers;
he will strike at your head,
while you strike at his heel."

The man called his wife Eve,
because she became the mother of all the living.

Psalm Ps 98:1, 2-3B, 3C-4
R. **Sing to the Lord a new song, for he has done marvelous deeds.**

Sing to the LORD a new song,
for he has done wondrous deeds;
His right hand has won victory for him,
his holy arm.
R. **Sing to the Lord a new song, for he has done marvelous deeds.**

The LORD has made his salvation known:
in the sight of the nations he has revealed his justice.
He has remembered his kindness and his faithfulness
toward the house of Israel.
R. **Sing to the Lord a new song, for he has done marvelous deeds.**

All the ends of the earth have seen
the salvation by our God.
Sing joyfully to the LORD, all you lands;
break into song; sing praise.

R. **Sing to the Lord a new song, for he has done marvelous deeds.**

2nd Reading Eph 1:3-6, 11-12
Brothers and sisters:
Blessed be the God and Father of our Lord Jesus Christ,
who has blessed us in Christ
with every spiritual blessing in the heavens,
as he chose us in him, before the foundation of the world,
to be holy and without blemish before him.
In love he destined us for adoption to himself through Jesus Christ,
in accord with the favor of his will,
for the praise of the glory of his grace
that he granted us in the beloved.

In him we were also chosen,
destined in accord with the purpose of the One
who accomplishes all things according to the intention of his will,
so that we might exist for the praise of his glory,
we who first hoped in Christ.

Gospel Lk 1:26-38
The angel Gabriel was sent from God
to a town of Galilee called Nazareth,
to a virgin betrothed to a man named Joseph,
of the house of David,
and the virgin's name was Mary.
And coming to her, he said,
"Hail, full of grace! The Lord is with you."

But she was greatly troubled at what was said and pondered what sort of greeting this might be.
Then the angel said to her,
"Do not be afraid, Mary,
for you have found favor with God.
Behold, you will conceive in your womb and bear a son,
and you shall name him Jesus.
He will be great and will be called Son of the Most High,
and the Lord God will give him the throne of David his father,
and he will rule over the house of Jacob forever,
and of his Kingdom there will be no end."
But Mary said to the angel,
"How can this be,
since I have no relations with a man?"
And the angel said to her in reply,
"The Holy Spirit will come upon you,
and the power of the Most High will overshadow you.
Therefore the child to be born
will be called holy, the Son of God.
And behold, Elizabeth, your relative,
has also conceived a son in her old age,
and this is the sixth month for her who was called barren;
for nothing will be impossible for God."
Mary said, "Behold, I am the handmaid of the Lord.
May it be done to me according to your word."
Then the angel departed from her.

"The Holy Spirit will come upon you, and the power of the most high will overshadow you." Lk 1:35

My pastor has been with our parish for 3 years and during that time the Lord has used him to breathe new life into our community. He came to us when we were hurting and the Lord used him to change our outlook and to rejuvenate us with his youthful spirit. He helped us discern God's vision for our parish and make things right again.

God has a vision for each of us. He has given us the gift of his Spirit to inspire us and to move us in his direction. Like Mary, we are moved in many ways by the grace of God. Like Mary, we are regular people, living regular lives, praying, reading scripture, and being changed by grace each day. We are ordinary people whom God has chosen to make extraordinary witnesses. In choosing us, God covers us with his Spirit. Through that same Spirit we are called to do little things with great love, but also to do great big things and to live for the greater glory of God. What are these great tasks? Well, the first is to work for a continuous conversion of our own heart, and then to strive to help those in need in the world around us. Our inspired "Yes" to God allows us to go out in faith to accomplish God's will and in doing so to join the choir of angels proclaiming Jesus's birth. And now my life song sings.

2nd Tuesday of Advent

1st Reading Is 40:1-11

Comfort, give comfort to my people,
says your God.
Speak tenderly to Jerusalem, and proclaim to her
that her service is at an end,
her guilt is expiated;
Indeed, she has received from the hand of the LORD
double for all her sins.

A voice cries out:
In the desert prepare the way of the LORD!
Make straight in the wasteland a highway for our God!
Every valley shall be filled in,
every mountain and hill shall be made low;
The rugged land shall be made a plain,
the rough country, a broad valley.
Then the glory of the LORD shall be revealed,
and all people shall see it together;
for the mouth of the LORD has spoken.

A voice says, "Cry out!"
I answer, "What shall I cry out?"
"All flesh is grass,
and all their glory like the flower of the field.
The grass withers, the flower wilts,
when the breath of the LORD blows upon it.
So then, the people is the grass.
Though the grass withers and the flower wilts,

the word of our God stands forever."

Go up onto a high mountain,
Zion, herald of glad tidings;
Cry out at the top of your voice,
Jerusalem, herald of good news!
Fear not to cry out
and say to the cities of Judah:
Here is your God!
Here comes with power
the Lord GOD,
who rules by his strong arm;
Here is his reward with him,
his recompense before him.
Like a shepherd he feeds his flock;
in his arms he gathers the lambs,
Carrying them in his bosom,
and leading the ewes with care.

Psalm Ps 96:1-2, 3 and 10C, 11-12, 13
R. **The Lord our God comes with power.**

Sing to the LORD a new song;
sing to the LORD, all you lands.
Sing to the LORD; bless his name;
announce his salvation, day after day.
R. **The Lord our God comes with power.**

Tell his glory among the nations;
among all peoples, his wondrous deeds.
Say among the nations:The LORD is king;
he governs the peoples with equity.
R. **The Lord our God comes with power.**

Let the heavens be glad and the earth rejoice;
let the sea and what fills it resound;
let the plains be joyful and all that is in them!
Then let all the trees of the forest rejoice.
R. **The Lord our God comes with power.**

They shall exult before the LORD, for he comes;
for he comes to rule the earth.
He shall rule the world with justice
and the peoples with his constancy.
R. **The Lord our God comes with power.**

Gospel Mt 18:12-14
Jesus said to his disciples:
"What is your opinion?
If a man has a hundred sheep and one of them goes astray,
will he not leave the ninety-nine in the hills
and go in search of the stray?
And if he finds it, amen, I say to you, he rejoices more over it
than over the ninety-nine that did not stray.
In just the same way, it is not the will of your heavenly Father
that one of these little ones be lost."

"And if he finds it, amen, I say to you, he rejoices." Mt 12:13

My friend, Deacon Jim, and I met 14 years ago on a Cursillo weekend. On that weekend he went from searching for something to allowing himself to be found. He recognized that God had changed his life and he asked the question: "What do I do now?" He changed from being the first person out of the church parking lot after Mass to a person who shared in the life of the community, and his life grew. In his wildest dreams he never thought that he would be led to the Deaconate program, or that he would make it through. This all happened because he allowed himself to be found. His example gives hope to us who need the courage to let God find us. And now my life song sings.

2nd Wednesday of Advent

1st Reading Is 40:25-31
To whom can you liken me as an equal?
says the Holy One.
Lift up your eyes on high
and see who has created these things:
He leads out their army and numbers them,
calling them all by name.
By his great might and the strength of his power
not one of them is missing!
Why, O Jacob, do you say,
and declare, O Israel,
"My way is hidden from the LORD,
and my right is disregarded by my God"?
Do you not know
or have you not heard?
The LORD is the eternal God,
creator of the ends of the earth.
He does not faint nor grow weary,
and his knowledge is beyond scrutiny.
He gives strength to the fainting;
for the weak he makes vigor abound.
Though young men faint and grow weary,
and youths stagger and fall,
They that hope in the LORD will renew their strength,
they will soar as with eagles' wings;
They will run and not grow weary,
walk and not grow faint.

Psalm Ps 103:1-2, 3-4, 8 and 10
R. **O bless the Lord, my soul!**

Bless the LORD, O my soul;
and all my being, bless his holy name.
Bless the LORD, O my soul,
and forget not all his benefits.
R. **O bless the Lord, my soul!**

He pardons all your iniquities,
he heals all your ills.
He redeems your life from destruction,
he crowns you with kindness and compassion.
R. **O bless the Lord, my soul!**

Merciful and gracious is the LORD,
slow to anger and abounding in kindness.
Not according to our sins does he deal with us,
nor does he requite us according to our crimes.
R. **O bless the Lord, my soul!**

Gospel Mt 11:28-30
Jesus said to the crowds:
"Come to me, all you who labor and are burdened,
and I will give you rest.
Take my yoke upon you and learn from me,
for I am meek and humble of heart;
and you will find rest for yourselves.
For my yoke is easy, and my burden light."

"Come to me all who labor and are burdened, and I will give you rest." Mt 11:28

When I was going through my divorce there came a day when it seemed that the whole world was working against me. I believed that everything that had gone wrong in my life was all because of me and that life had been nothing but one disappointment after another. I was at the point of considering taking my own life. Then God planted a seed in me. It was a seed that soon sprouted and allowed me the strength and courage to go on. That seed was: "Come to me, and I will give you rest."

This season you may not find the perfect gift for a family member or friend, but you do have the opportunity to plant words of encouragement and kindness. Plant the seed of Christ, and see what the Spirit does with it. And now my life song sings.

2nd Thursday of Advent

1st Reading Zec 2:14-17
Sing and rejoice, O daughter Zion!
See, I am coming to dwell among you, says the LORD.
Many nations shall join themselves to the LORD on that day,
and they shall be his people,
and he will dwell among you,
and you shall know that the LORD of hosts has sent me to you.
The LORD will possess Judah as his portion in the holy land,
and he will again choose Jerusalem.
Silence, all mankind, in the presence of the LORD!
For he stirs forth from his holy dwelling.

Psalm Judith 13:B, C, D, &E, and 19
R. **You are the highest honor of our race.**

Blessed are you, daughter, by the Most High God,
above all the women on earth;
and blessed be the LORD God,
the creator of heaven and earth.
R. **You are the highest honor of our race.**

Your deed of hope will never be forgotten
by those who tell of the might of God.
R. **You are the highest honor of our race.**

Gospel Lk 1:39-47
Mary set out
and traveled to the hill country in haste
to a town of Judah,
where she entered the house of Zechariah
and greeted Elizabeth.
When Elizabeth heard Mary's greeting,
the infant leaped in her womb,
and Elizabeth, filled with the Holy Spirit,
cried out in a loud voice and said,
"Most blessed are you among women,
and blessed is the fruit of your womb.
And how does this happen to me,
that the mother of my Lord should come to me?
For at the moment the sound of your greeting
reached my ears,
the infant in my womb leaped for joy.
Blessed are you who believed
that what was spoken to you by the Lord
would be fulfilled."

And Mary said:
"My soul proclaims the greatness of the Lord;
my spirit rejoices in God my savior."

"Blessed are you who believed that what was spoken would be fulfilled." Lk 1:45

When my friend Oliver was diagnosed with cancer he and his wife did not give in to despair, but chose to face it head on. They fought it with the support and prayers of a loving community. Today Oliver is vibrant, joyful, full of life and cancer-free. He has become an example for our church community not just because of his faith, but because of the impact that he has on the lives that he touches.

Maybe you have had a challenge similar to Oliver's. Are you allowing others to support you by their prayers? God has created us so that we can lean on one another. When we share our struggles, we are open to learning the "overcomer" attitude. Overcomers believe that all things are possible as we follow the same road that Mary walked, the road that leads us to Christ, the light of the world. And now my life song sings.

2nd Friday of Advent

1st Reading Is 48:17-19
Thus says the LORD, your redeemer,
the Holy One of Israel:
I, the LORD, your God,
teach you what is for your good,
and lead you on the way you should go.
If you would hearken to my commandments,
your prosperity would be like a river,
and your vindication like the waves of the sea;
Your descendants would be like the sand,
and those born of your stock like its grains,
Their name never cut off
or blotted out from my presence.

Psalm Ps 1:1-2, 3, 4 and 6
R. **Those who follow you, Lord, will have the light of life.**

Blessed the man who follows not
the counsel of the wicked
Nor walks in the way of sinners,
nor sits in the company of the insolent,
But delights in the law of the LORD
and meditates on his law day and night.
R. **Those who follow you, Lord, will have the light of life.**

He is like a tree
planted near running water,
That yields its fruit in due season,
and whose leaves never fade.

Whatever he does, prospers.
R. **Those who follow you, Lord, will have the light of life.**

Not so the wicked, not so;
they are like chaff which the wind drives away.
For the LORD watches over the way of the just,
but the way of the wicked vanishes.
R. **Those who follow you, Lord, will have the light of life.**

Gospel Mt 11:16-19
Jesus said to the crowds:
"To what shall I compare this generation?
It is like children who sit in marketplaces and call to one another,
'We played the flute for you, but you did not dance,
we sang a dirge but you did not mourn.'
For John came neither eating nor drinking, and they said,
'He is possessed by a demon.'
The Son of Man came eating and drinking and they said,
'Look, he is a glutton and a drunkard,
a friend of tax collectors and sinners.'
But wisdom is vindicated by her works."

"Wisdom is vindicated by her works." Mt 11:19

Wisdom is not always found in books or college campuses. My friend Warren is proof of that. Much of his wisdom has come from revelation. Through studying scripture and praying with it, he has spoken many words of wisdom that to me and others. Every week he has a different message that many reflect on. He sends it out via email on a Monday but also on every other day of the week, so that those who read it have an opportunity to reflect deeply on it and to make it a part of their daily lives. Through the repetitive nature of its presentation, the wise word of God spoken through him strengthens, encourages, and helps others to find hope and joy in the reality that comes with living a life on purpose.

In the same way we have gained knowledge in our own lives – acquired wisdom – and we can choose to use this knowledge to help others. We each have some piece of wisdom to contribute and we do not need a degree, a certificate, or a license to do so. All we need is faith in God and the desire to share our wisdom and knowledge with others. He has given us the ability to lead others on the desert road of life so that they also may come with us to Bethlehem to see the child who is our King. And now my life song sings.

2nd Saturday of Advent

1st Reading Sir 48:1-4, 9-11
In those days,
like a fire there appeared the prophet Elijah
whose words were as a flaming furnace.
Their staff of bread he shattered,
in his zeal he reduced them to straits;
By the Lord's word he shut up the heavens
and three times brought down fire.
How awesome are you, Elijah, in your wondrous deeds!
Whose glory is equal to yours?
You were taken aloft in a whirlwind of fire,
in a chariot with fiery horses.
You were destined, it is written, in time to come
to put an end to wrath before the day of the LORD,
To turn back the hearts of fathers toward their sons,
and to re-establish the tribes of Jacob.
Blessed is he who shall have seen you
and who falls asleep in your friendship.

Psalm Ps 80:2a, c, and 3b, 15-16, 18-19
R. **Lord, make us turn to you; let us see your face and we shall be saved.**

O shepherd of Israel, hearken,
From your throne upon the cherubim, shine forth.
Rouse your power.

R. **Lord, make us turn to you; let us see your face and we shall be saved.**

Once again, O LORD of hosts,
look down from heaven, and see;
Take care of this vine,
and protect what your right hand has planted
the son of man whom you yourself made strong.
R. **Lord, make us turn to you; let us see your face and we shall be saved.**

May your help be with the man of your right hand,
with the son of man whom you yourself made strong.
Then we will no more withdraw from you;
give us new life, and we will call upon your name.
R. **Lord, make us turn to you; let us see your face and we shall be saved.**

Gospel Mt 17:9a, 10-13
As they were coming down from the mountain,
the disciples asked Jesus,
"Why do the scribes say that Elijah must come first?"
He said in reply, "Elijah will indeed come and restore all things;
but I tell you that Elijah has already come,
and they did not recognize him but did to him whatever they pleased.
So also will the Son of Man suffer at their hands."

Then the disciples understood
that he was speaking to them of John the Baptist.

"Come and restore all things." Mt 17:11

I haven't been the healthiest person during my life time. When my transplanted pancreas failed I went through the necessary steps to ensure that I could be placed back on the list for another transplant. I would be lying to you if I said that I don't get frustrated sometimes and question why this happened. Acceptance is the path that I must choose. I realize that even if I have to take insulin shots for the rest of my life, it is not a personal attack against me but an invitation to experience even greater moments of God's grace in my life.

We are going to question some of the things that occur in our lives. Our struggles teach us the virtues of patience, trust, and faith. God's purpose is always to increase in us all things that are good. We will struggle because that is a part of the spiritual life. The things that come from those struggles are that we witness the restoration of new life and the rebirth of the Christ Child in our hearts. And now my life song sings.

3rd Sunday of Advent

1st Reading Is 35:1-6A, 10
The desert and the parched land will exult;
the steppe will rejoice and bloom.
They will bloom with abundant flowers,
and rejoice with joyful song.
The glory of Lebanon will be given to them,
the splendor of Carmel and Sharon;
they will see the glory of the LORD,
the splendor of our God.
Strengthen the hands that are feeble,
make firm the knees that are weak,
say to those whose hearts are frightened:
Be strong, fear not!
Here is your God,
he comes with vindication;
with divine recompense
he comes to save you.
Then will the eyes of the blind be opened,
the ears of the deaf be cleared;
then will the lame leap like a stag,
then the tongue of the mute will sing.

Those whom the LORD has ransomed will return
and enter Zion singing,
crowned with everlasting joy;
they will meet with joy and gladness,
sorrow and mourning will flee.

Psalm Ps:146:6-7, 8-9, 9-10
R. **Lord, come and save us.**

The LORD God keeps faith forever,
secures justice for the oppressed,
gives food to the hungry.
The LORD sets captives free.
R. **Lord, come and save us.**

The LORD gives sight to the blind;
the LORD raises up those who were bowed down.
The LORD loves the just;
the LORD protects strangers.
R. **Lord, come and save us.**

The fatherless and the widow he sustains,
but the way of the wicked he thwarts.
The LORD shall reign forever;
your God, O Zion, through all generations.
R. **Lord, come and save us.**

2nd Reading James 5:7-10
Be patient, brothers and sisters,
until the coming of the Lord.
See how the farmer waits for the precious fruit of the earth,
being patient with it
until it receives the early and the late rains.
You too must be patient.
Make your hearts firm,
because the coming of the Lord is at hand.
Do not complain, brothers and sisters, about one another,
that you may not be judged.

Behold, the Judge is standing before the gates.
Take as an example of hardship and patience,
brothers and sisters,
the prophets who spoke in the name of the Lord.

Gospel Mt 11:2-11
When John the Baptist heard in prison of the works of the Christ,
he sent his disciples to Jesus with this question,
"Are you the one who is to come,
or should we look for another?"
Jesus said to them in reply,
"Go and tell John what you hear and see:
the blind regain their sight,
the lame walk,
lepers are cleansed,
the deaf hear,
the dead are raised,
and the poor have the good news proclaimed to them.
And blessed is the one who takes no offense at me."

As they were going off,
Jesus began to speak to the crowds about John,
"What did you go out to the desert to see?
A reed swayed by the wind?
Then what did you go out to see?
Someone dressed in fine clothing?
Those who wear fine clothing are in royal palaces.
Then why did you go out? To see a prophet?
Yes, I tell you, and more than a prophet.

This is the one about whom it is written:
Behold, I am sending my messenger ahead of you;
he will prepare your way before you.
Amen, I say to you,
among those born of women
there has been none greater than John the Baptist;
yet the least in the kingdom of heaven is greater than he."

"The blind regain their sight, the lame walk, lepers are cleansed, the deaf hear, the dead are raised, and the poor have the good news proclaimed to them." Mt 11:5

My friend Ray had a long and hard battle against cancer. As the disease continued to take more and more control of his body, his mind began to fade in and out of reality. I visited him at his home and I could see his struggle and how his body was giving in to the death that was to come. I visited for a while and he spoke in audible words and sentences that had no meaning to them. As I was leaving he got up to walk out with me. As we said goodbye he was completely coherent and in the moment. I told him that our entire community was praying for him and that we loved him. He responded with the words: "I love you too." Two days later Ray won his battle against cancer and went home to the Lord.

We can never predict when the good news of Christ will be proclaimed to us. If we think about it, we have all had encounters with God's grace. In grace-filled moments we see again, we walk, we are cleansed, we hear, we are raised, and we see the good news lived out in our presence. Great things happen when God mixes with us, and through these great things we encounter all these blessings of the Christ child wrapped up in a nice package placed in a manger. And now my life song sings.

3rd Monday of Advent

1st Reading Numbers 24:2-7, 15-17A
When Balaam raised his eyes and saw Israel
encamped, tribe by tribe,
the spirit of God came upon him,
and he gave voice to his oracle:

The utterance of Balaam, son of Beor,
the utterance of a man whose eye is true,
The utterance of one who hears what God says,
and knows what the Most High knows,
Of one who sees what the Almighty sees,
enraptured, and with eyes unveiled:
How goodly are your tents, O Jacob;
your encampments, O Israel!
They are like gardens beside a stream,
like the cedars planted by the LORD.
His wells shall yield free-flowing waters,
he shall have the sea within reach;
His king shall rise higher,
and his royalty shall be exalted.

Then Balaam gave voice to his oracle:

The utterance of Balaam, son of Beor,
the utterance of the man whose eye is true,
The utterance of one who hears what God says,
and knows what the Most High knows,
Of one who sees what the Almighty sees,
enraptured, and with eyes unveiled.
I see him, though not now;
I behold him, though not near:

A star shall advance from Jacob,
and a staff shall rise from Israel.

Psalm Ps 25:4-5 AB, 6 and 7 BC, 8-9
R. **Teach me your ways, O Lord.**

Your ways, O LORD, make known to me;
teach me your paths,
Guide me in your truth and teach me,
for you are God my savior.
R. **Teach me your ways, O Lord.**

Remember that your compassion, O LORD,
and your kindness are from of old.
In your kindness remember me,
because of your goodness, O LORD.
R. **Teach me your ways, O Lord.**

Good and upright is the LORD;
thus he shows sinners the way.
He guides the humble to justice,
he teaches the humble his way.
R. **Teach me your ways, O Lord.**

Gospel Mt 21:23-27
When Jesus had come into the temple area,
the chief priests and the elders of the people
approached him
as he was teaching and said,
"By what authority are you doing these things?
And who gave you this authority?"
Jesus said to them in reply,
"I shall ask you one question, and if you answer

it for me,
then I shall tell you by what authority I do these things.
Where was John's baptism from?
Was it of heavenly or of human origin?"
They discussed this among themselves and said,
"If we say 'Of heavenly origin,' he will say to us,
'Then why did you not believe him?'
But if we say, 'Of human origin,' we fear the crowd,
for they all regard John as a prophet."
So they said to Jesus in reply, "We do not know."
He himself said to them,
"Neither shall I tell you by what authority I do these things."

"By what authority are you doing these things?" Mt 21:23

When my friend Fr. Peter came to our parish as its new pastor he made changes – removing the choir loft, changing the phone system, and some other things. He brought fresh and innovative ideas that enhanced the life of the community. There was also resistance that came with these changes. In time our community saw the wisdom in the changes that took place and we grew stronger as a community of faith.

There is always a need for change, in body, in spirit and in community. The question will arise, "By whose authority are these things taking place?" Mother Theresa, Pope John Paul II, and Martin Luther King, Jr., are just a few of the leaders who saw the need for change and went about accomplishing that change, despite opposition. They obeyed God, and relied on his authority to change the world. We, too, can obey God and rely on his authority to change ourselves, our families, and our communities not as the world sees fit, but as God sees fit. Our world has already changed because we have knelt down to worship at the cradle of a child who was born to be savior of the world. And now my life song sings.

3rd Tuesday of Advent

1st Reading Gn 49:2, 8-10
Jacob called his sons and said to them:
"Assemble and listen, sons of Jacob,
listen to Israel, your father.

"You, Judah, shall your brothers praise
–your hand on the neck of your enemies;
the sons of your father shall bow down to you.
Judah, like a lion's whelp,
you have grown up on prey, my son.
He crouches like a lion recumbent,
the king of beasts–who would dare rouse him?
The scepter shall never depart from Judah,
or the mace from between his legs,
While tribute is brought to him,
and he receives the people's homage."

Psalm Ps 72:1-2, 3-4b, 7-8, 17
R. **Justice shall flourish in his time, and fullness of peace for ever.**

O God, with your judgment endow the king,
and with your justice, the king's son;
He shall govern your people with justice
and your afflicted ones with judgment.
R. **Justice shall flourish in his time, and fullness of peace for ever.**

The mountains shall yield peace for the people,
and the hills justice.
He shall defend the afflicted among the people,

save the children of the poor.
R. **Justice shall flourish in his time, and fullness of peace for ever.**

Justice shall flower in his days,
and profound peace, till the moon be no more.
May he rule from sea to sea,
and from the River to the ends of the earth.
R. **Justice shall flourish in his time, and fullness of peace for ever.**

May his name be blessed forever;
as long as the sun his name shall remain.
In him shall all the tribes of the earth be blessed;
all the nations shall proclaim his happiness.
R. **Justice shall flourish in his time, and fullness of peace for ever.**

Gospel Mt 1:1-17
The book of the genealogy of Jesus Christ,
the son of David, the son of Abraham.

Abraham became the father of Isaac,
Isaac the father of Jacob,
Jacob the father of Judah and his brothers.
Judah became the father of Perez and Zerah,
whose mother was Tamar.
Perez became the father of Hezron,
Hezron the father of Ram,
Ram the father of Amminadab.
Amminadab became the father of Nahshon,
Nahshon the father of Salmon,
Salmon the father of Boaz,

whose mother was Rahab.
Boaz became the father of Obed,
whose mother was Ruth.
Obed became the father of Jesse,
Jesse the father of David the king.

David became the father of Solomon,
whose mother had been the wife of Uriah.
Solomon became the father of Rehoboam,
Rehoboam the father of Abijah,
Abijah the father of Asaph.
Asaph became the father of Jehoshaphat,
Jehoshaphat the father of Joram,
Joram the father of Uzziah.
Uzziah became the father of Jotham,
Jotham the father of Ahaz,
Ahaz the father of Hezekiah.
Hezekiah became the father of Manasseh,
Manasseh the father of Amos,
Amos the father of Josiah.
Josiah became the father of Jechoniah and his brothers
at the time of the Babylonian exile.

After the Babylonian exile,
Jechoniah became the father of Shealtiel,
Shealtiel the father of Zerubbabel,
Zerubbabel the father of Abiud.
Abiud became the father of Eliakim,
Eliakim the father of Azor,
Azor the father of Zadok.
Zadok became the father of Achim,
Achim the father of Eliud,

Eliud the father of Eleazar.
Eleazar became the father of Matthan,
Matthan the father of Jacob,
Jacob the father of Joseph, the husband of Mary.
Of her was born Jesus who is called the Christ.

Thus the total number of generations
from Abraham to David
is fourteen generations;
from David to the Babylonian exile, fourteen generations;
from the Babylonian exile to the Christ,
fourteen generations.

"From the Babylonian exile to the Messiah." Mt 1:17

I have a friend who has moved from darkness to light. She once abused drugs and lived a shattered life but when the Lord caught up to her he made her strong enough to turn her life around. She found the light of Christ and she refuses to let it go. She now is an addictions consoler, witnessing to others and helping them to become free from the darkness that controls their lives and to return from their exiled existence apart from God.

We too have experienced darkness in our lives, times when we lived through our own "Babylonian exile." But Jesus was born into the world to provide us with the hope of recovery from all of our addictions and experiences of exile. Like my friend, we are now children of the light, blessed and highly favored, so that we too can be witnesses of hope to a world that lives in darkness, far from God. And now my life song sings.

3rd Wednesday of Advent

1st Reading Jer 23:5-8

Behold, the days are coming, says the LORD,
when I will raise up a righteous shoot to David;
As king he shall reign and govern wisely,
he shall do what is just and right in the land.
In his days Judah shall be saved,
Israel shall dwell in security.
This is the name they give him:
"The LORD our justice."

Therefore, the days will come, says the LORD,
when they shall no longer say, "As the LORD lives,
who brought the children of Israel out of the land of Egypt";
but rather, "As the LORD lives,
who brought the descendants of the house of Israel
up from the land of the north"–
and from all the lands to which I banished them;
they shall again live on their own land.

Psalm Ps 72:1-2, 12-13, 18-19

R. **Justice shall flourish in his time, and fullness of peace for ever.**

O God, with your judgment endow the king,
and with your justice, the king's son;
He shall govern your people with justice
and your afflicted ones with judgment.

R. **Justice shall flourish in his time, and fullness of peace for ever.**

For he shall rescue the poor when he cries out,
and the afflicted when he has no one to help him.
He shall have pity for the lowly and the poor;
the lives of the poor he shall save.
R. **Justice shall flourish in his time, and fullness of peace for ever.**

Blessed be the LORD, the God of Israel,
who alone does wondrous deeds.
And blessed forever be his glorious name;
may the whole earth be filled with his glory.
R. **Justice shall flourish in his time, and fullness of peace for ever.**

Gospel Mt 1:18-25
This is how the birth of Jesus Christ came about.
When his mother Mary was betrothed to Joseph,
but before they lived together,
she was found with child through the Holy Spirit.
Joseph her husband, since he was a righteous man,
yet unwilling to expose her to shame,
decided to divorce her quietly.
Such was his intention when, behold,
the angel of the Lord appeared to him in a dream and said,
"Joseph, son of David,
do not be afraid to take Mary your wife into

your home.
For it is through the Holy Spirit
that this child has been conceived in her.
She will bear a son and you are to name him
Jesus,
because he will save his people from their sins."
All this took place to fulfill
what the Lord had said through the prophet:

Behold, the virgin shall be with child and bear a son,
and they shall name him Emmanuel,

which means "God is with us."
When Joseph awoke,
he did as the angel of the Lord had commanded
him
and took his wife into his home.
He had no relations with her until she bore a
son,
and he named him Jesus.

"It is through the Holy Spirit that this child has been conceived." Mt 18 19

My friends La'Mont and Kelli are the ideal couple. They have been built up in faith and grounded in love. They are true examples of married life to their community and many look up to them. The Lord has blessed them in many ways but they have no children. Even though childless, they have become spiritual parents to many people, including myself. Their advice and love has helped me through trying times so that I could regain focus on the important things of life. Trusting God, they have conceived – and raised – many spiritual children.

Like Kelli and La'Mont we need to stay focused on the sunny side of life. We need to appreciate what we have and not dwell on what we have not. The Holy Spirit works in mysterious ways to give us what we need. Christ wasn't just born once, but he is still being born in those who accept the Spirit's invitation to begin a life of grace. And now my life song sings.

3rd Thursday of Advent

1st Reading Judges 13:2-7, 24-25A

There was a certain man from Zorah, of the clan of the Danites,
whose name was Manoah.
His wife was barren and had borne no children.
An angel of the LORD appeared to the woman and said to her,
"Though you are barren and have had no children,
yet you will conceive and bear a son.
Now, then, be careful to take no wine or strong drink
and to eat nothing unclean.
As for the son you will conceive and bear,
no razor shall touch his head,
for this boy is to be consecrated to God from the womb.
It is he who will begin the deliverance of Israel from the power of the Philistines."

The woman went and told her husband,
"A man of God came to me;
he had the appearance of an angel of God, terrible indeed.
I did not ask him where he came from, nor did he tell me his name.
But he said to me,
'You will be with child and will bear a son.
So take neither wine nor strong drink, and eat nothing unclean.
For the boy shall be consecrated to God from

the womb,
until the day of his death.'"

The woman bore a son and named him Samson.
The boy grew up and the LORD blessed him;
the Spirit of the LORD stirred him.

Psalm Ps 71:3-4A, 5-6 A B, 16-17
R. **My mouth shall be filled with your praise, and I will sing your glory!**

Be my rock of refuge,
a stronghold to give me safety,
for you are my rock and my fortress.
O my God, rescue me from the hand of the wicked.
R. **My mouth shall be filled with your praise, and I will sing your glory!**

For you are my hope, O LORD;
my trust, O God, from my youth.
On you I depend from birth;
from my mother's womb you are my strength.
R. **My mouth shall be filled with your praise, and I will sing your glory!**

I will treat of the mighty works of the LORD;
O God, I will tell of your singular justice.
O God, you have taught me from my youth,
and till the present I proclaim your wondrous deeds.
R. **My mouth shall be filled with your praise, and I will sing your glory!**

Gospel Lk 1:5-25
In the days of Herod, King of Judea,
there was a priest named Zechariah
of the priestly division of Abijah;
his wife was from the daughters of Aaron,
and her name was Elizabeth.
Both were righteous in the eyes of God,
observing all the commandments
and ordinances of the Lord blamelessly.
But they had no child, because Elizabeth was barren
and both were advanced in years.

Once when he was serving as priest
in his division's turn before God,
according to the practice of the priestly service,
he was chosen by lot
to enter the sanctuary of the Lord to burn incense.
Then, when the whole assembly of the people was praying outside
at the hour of the incense offering,
the angel of the Lord appeared to him,
standing at the right of the altar of incense.
Zechariah was troubled by what he saw, and fear came upon him.

But the angel said to him, "Do not be afraid, Zechariah,
because your prayer has been heard.
Your wife Elizabeth will bear you a son,
and you shall name him John.

And you will have joy and gladness,
and many will rejoice at his birth,
for he will be great in the sight of the Lord.
He will drink neither wine nor strong drink.
He will be filled with the Holy Spirit even from his mother's womb,
and he will turn many of the children of Israel to the Lord their God.
He will go before him in the spirit and power of Elijah
to turn the hearts of fathers toward children
and the disobedient to the understanding of the righteous,
to prepare a people fit for the Lord."

Then Zechariah said to the angel,
"How shall I know this?
For I am an old man, and my wife is advanced in years."
And the angel said to him in reply,
"I am Gabriel, who stand before God.
I was sent to speak to you and to announce to you this good news.
But now you will be speechless and unable to talk
until the day these things take place,
because you did not believe my words,
which will be fulfilled at their proper time."
Meanwhile the people were waiting for Zechariah
and were amazed that he stayed so long in the sanctuary.
But when he came out, he was unable to speak

to them,
and they realized that he had seen a vision in the sanctuary.
He was gesturing to them but remained mute.

Then, when his days of ministry were completed, he went home.

After this time his wife Elizabeth conceived,
and she went into seclusion for five months, saying,
"So has the Lord done for me at a time when he has seen fit
to take away my disgrace before others."

"Believe my words which will be fulfilled at the proper time." Lk 1:20

My friends Dan and Angie have been together since high school. In their married life they always wanted a family but they could not have children. They entered the process of adoption, and after many anxious days Maria Terese entered their life in October of 2004. Joseph followed in 2008. Their faith gave them hope so that they could overcome those moments of doubt and now their dreams have been realized according to the Lord's time-table.

Today God is working on something that is just for you. We just need to remain faithful and hope in his promise until its proper time arrives. Advent is the proper time to witness the birth of Love. Keep watching and waiting – don't miss it. And now my life song sings.

3rd Friday of Advent

1st Reading Is 7:10-14
The LORD spoke to Ahaz:
Ask for a sign from the LORD, your God;
let it be deep as the nether world, or high as the sky!
But Ahaz answered,
"I will not ask! I will not tempt the LORD!"
Then Isaiah said:
Listen, O house of David!
Is it not enough for you to weary men,
must you also weary my God?
Therefore the Lord himself will give you this sign:
the virgin shall conceive and bear a son,
and shall name him Emmanuel.

Psalm Ps 24:1-2, 3-4 A and B, 5-6
R. **Let the Lord enter; he is the king of glory.**

The LORD's are the earth and its fullness;
the world and those who dwell in it.
For he founded it upon the seas
and established it upon the rivers.
R. **Let the Lord enter; he is the king of glory.**

Who can ascend the mountain of the LORD?
or who may stand in his holy place?
He whose hands are sinless, whose heart is clean,
who desires not what is vain.
R. **Let the Lord enter; he is the king of glory.**

He shall receive a blessing from the LORD,
a reward from God his savior.
Such is the race that seeks for him,
that seeks the face of the God of Jacob.
R. **Let the Lord enter; he is the king of glory.**

Gospel Lk 1:26-38
In the sixth month,
the angel Gabriel was sent from God
to a town of Galilee called Nazareth,
to a virgin betrothed to a man named Joseph,
of the house of David,
and the virgin's name was Mary.
And coming to her, he said,
"Hail, full of grace! The Lord is with you."
But she was greatly troubled at what was said
and pondered what sort of greeting this might be.
Then the angel said to her,
"Do not be afraid, Mary,
for you have found favor with God.
Behold, you will conceive in your womb and bear a son,
and you shall name him Jesus.
He will be great and will be called Son of the Most High,
and the Lord God will give him the throne of David his father,
and he will rule over the house of Jacob forever,
and of his Kingdom there will be no end."

But Mary said to the angel,

"How can this be,
since I have no relations with a man?"
And the angel said to her in reply,
"The Holy Spirit will come upon you,
and the power of the Most High will overshadow you.
Therefore the child to be born
will be called holy, the Son of God.
And behold, Elizabeth, your relative,
has also conceived a son in her old age,
and this is the sixth month for her who was called barren;
for nothing will be impossible for God."

Mary said, "Behold, I am the handmaid of the Lord.
May it be done to me according to your word."
Then the angel departed from her.

"Son of the Most High." Lk 1:32

The early years of my high school education were not the greatest years of my life. I was someone who did not consider himself handsome or intelligent. I was an easy target for others to push around and bad things were said about me. I was afraid to do anything about it and soon I began to believe all the bad things and questioned how God could love someone whom no one else could. I never really considered myself God's child until one weekend when someone sat me down and explained God's love to me. For so long I had thought that God was running from me when in reality I was running from him. That weekend things changed because I came to believe that I was worthy to be called a son of the most high.

We are all worthy of that title. God so loved us that he breathed us into existence and gave us a life with purpose. Our acceptance of God and of ourselves is the first step in believing that we are, indeed, God's children, sons and daughters of the most high. And now my life song sings.

3rd Saturday of Advent

1st Reading Song 2:8-14
Hark! my lover–here he comes
springing across the mountains,
leaping across the hills.
My lover is like a gazelle
or a young stag.
Here he stands behind our wall,
gazing through the windows,
peering through the lattices.
My lover speaks; he says to me,
"Arise, my beloved, my dove, my beautiful one,
and come!
"For see, the winter is past,
the rains are over and gone.
The flowers appear on the earth,
the time of pruning the vines has come,
and the song of the dove is heard in our land.
The fig tree puts forth its figs,
and the vines, in bloom, give forth fragrance.
Arise, my beloved, my beautiful one,
and come!

"O my dove in the clefts of the rock,
in the secret recesses of the cliff,
Let me see you,
let me hear your voice,
For your voice is sweet,
and you are lovely."

Psalm Ps 33:2-3, 11-12, 20-21

R. **Exult, you just, in the Lord! Sing to him a new song.**

Give thanks to the LORD on the harp;
with the ten-stringed lyre chant his praises.
Sing to him a new song;
pluck the strings skillfully, with shouts of gladness.
R. **Exult, you just, in the Lord! Sing to him a new song.**

But the plan of the LORD stands forever;
the design of his heart, through all generations.
Blessed the nation whose God is the LORD,
the people he has chosen for his own inheritance.
R. **Exult, you just, in the Lord! Sing to him a new song.**

Our soul waits for the LORD,
who is our help and our shield,
For in him our hearts rejoice;
in his holy name we trust.
R. **Exult, you just, in the Lord! Sing to him a new song.**

Gospel Lk 1:39-45
Mary set out in those days
and traveled to the hill country in haste
to a town of Judah,
where she entered the house of Zechariah
and greeted Elizabeth.
When Elizabeth heard Mary's greeting,

the infant leaped in her womb,
and Elizabeth, filled with the Holy Spirit,
cried out in a loud voice and said,
"Most blessed are you among women,
and blessed is the fruit of your womb.
And how does this happen to me,
that the mother of my Lord should come to me?
For at the moment the sound of your greeting
reached my ears,
the infant in my womb leaped for joy.
Blessed are you who believed
that what was spoken to you by the Lord
would be fulfilled."

"For at the moment the sound of your greeting reached my ears the infant in my womb leaped for joy." Lk 1:44

In 1988 and in 2005 my parents and my brothers enjoyed a trip to the village where my grandparents grew up in Oberammergau, Germany. Both times I was unable to go because of reasons beyond my control. In 2010 I got my chance to go to that same village and witness the Passion play that has been put on by the villagers every 10 years since 1634. For the whole day I experienced many feelings of joy, fulfillment, and tears. From being at the pottery shop where my great-grandfather worked to visiting my grandparents' gravesite, all things were life giving to me. The greatest experience was when I was walking through the village, looked in one of the shop windows and saw a picture of my grandmother. My heart leapt for joy, I caught my breath, and I cried and remembered.

We all have had times of joyful remembrance in our own lives. We remember weddings, births, holidays and close moments with friends and family. But all these moments are nothing compared to the joy of Elizabeth when she came into the presence of the unborn savior of the world. She had been waiting her whole life for this moment, not even knowing if it would come. We each have experiences, moments, and instances when the grace of God completely fills us and causes us to leap for joy like Edwin Moses leaping hurdles. We too are joyful because our savior is near. And now my life song sings.

4th Sunday of Advent

1st Reading Is 7:10-14
The LORD spoke to Ahaz, saying:
Ask for a sign from the LORD, your God;
let it be deep as the netherworld, or high as the sky!
But Ahaz answered,
"I will not ask! I will not tempt the LORD!"
Then Isaiah said:
Listen, O house of David!
Is it not enough for you to weary people,
must you also weary my God?
Therefore the Lord himself will give you this sign:
the virgin shall conceive, and bear a son,
and shall name him Emmanuel.

Psalm Ps 24:1-2,3-4.5-6
R. **Let the Lord enter; he is king of glory.**

The LORD's are the earth and its fullness;
the world and those who dwell in it.
For he founded it upon the seas
and established it upon the rivers.
R. **Let the Lord enter; he is king of glory.**

Who can ascend the mountain of the LORD?
or who may stand in his holy place?
One whose hands are sinless, whose heart is clean,
who desires not what is vain.
R. **Let the Lord enter; he is king of glory.**

He shall receive a blessing from the LORD,
a reward from God his savior.
Such is the race that seeks for him,
that seeks the face of the God of Jacob.
R. **Let the Lord enter; he is king of glory.**

2nd Reading Rom 1:1-7
Paul, a slave of Christ Jesus,
called to be an apostle and set apart for the gospel of God,
which he promised previously through his prophets in the holy Scriptures,
the gospel about his Son, descended from David according to the flesh,
but established as Son of God in power
according to the Spirit of holiness
through resurrection from the dead, Jesus Christ our Lord.
Through him we have received the grace of apostleship,
to bring about the obedience of faith,
for the sake of his name, among all the Gentiles,
among whom are you also, who are called to belong to Jesus Christ;
to all the beloved of God in Rome, called to be holy.
Grace to you and peace from God our Father
and the Lord Jesus Christ.

Gospel Mt 1:18-24
This is how the birth of Jesus Christ came about.
When his mother Mary was betrothed to Joseph,

but before they lived together,
she was found with child through the Holy Spirit.
Joseph her husband, since he was a righteous man,
yet unwilling to expose her to shame,
decided to divorce her quietly.
Such was his intention when, behold,
the angel of the Lord appeared to him in a dream and said,
"Joseph, son of David,
do not be afraid to take Mary your wife into your home.
For it is through the Holy Spirit
that this child has been conceived in her.
She will bear a son and you are to name him Jesus,
because he will save his people from their sins."
All this took place to fulfill what the Lord had said through the prophet:
Behold, the virgin shall conceive and bear a son,
and they shall name him Emmanuel,
which means "God is with us."
When Joseph awoke,
he did as the angel of the Lord had commanded him
and took his wife into his home.

"All of this took place to fulfill what the Lord has said." Mt 1:22

When I look at my life I see the ordeals that I have been through, yet Christ lives on.

From being born short in stature to having a disease that could have taken my life, Christ lives on. From marriage to divorce to living again, Christ lives on. From big mistakes to even bigger forgiveness, Christ lives on. Faith is the reason I have come this far and made it through. Without the presence of an all-loving God in my life, there would be no reason for me to continue. He has been my hope, my joy, and my everlasting.

Just because we walk by faith doesn't mean that we aren't going to have struggles in our lives. There are going to be times when we lack faith or understanding. Despite the world's imperfection and the sins of humanity, there is a divine master plan that has been instituted for our salvation. We are road tested and tough Christians who have survived and persevered. We will fulfill God's will and accomplish what the Lord had commanded. And now my life song sings.

4th Monday of Advent

1st Reading Mal 3:1-4, 23-24
Thus says the Lord GOD:
Lo, I am sending my messenger
to prepare the way before me;
And suddenly there will come to the temple
the LORD whom you seek,
And the messenger of the covenant whom you desire.
Yes, he is coming, says the LORD of hosts.
But who will endure the day of his coming?
And who can stand when he appears?
For he is like the refiner's fire,
or like the fuller's lye.
He will sit refining and purifying silver,
and he will purify the sons of Levi,
Refining them like gold or like silver
that they may offer due sacrifice to the LORD.
Then the sacrifice of Judah and Jerusalem
will please the LORD,
as in the days of old, as in years gone by.

Lo, I will send you
Elijah, the prophet,
Before the day of the LORD comes,
the great and terrible day,
To turn the hearts of the fathers to their children,
and the hearts of the children to their fathers,
Lest I come and strike
the land with doom.

Psalm Ps 25:4-5AB, 8-9, 10 and 14

R. **Lift up your heads and see; your redemption is near at hand.**

Your ways, O LORD, make known to me;
teach me your paths,
Guide me in your truth and teach me,
for you are God my savior.
R. **Lift up your heads and see; your redemption is near at hand.**

Good and upright is the LORD;
thus he shows sinners the way.
He guides the humble to justice,
he teaches the humble his way.
R. **Lift up your heads and see; your redemption is near at hand.**

All the paths of the LORD are kindness and constancy
toward those who keep his covenant and his decrees.
The friendship of the LORD is with those who fear him,
and his covenant, for their instruction.
R. **Lift up your heads and see; your redemption is near at hand.**

Gospel Lk 1:57-66

When the time arrived for Elizabeth to have her child
she gave birth to a son.
Her neighbors and relatives heard
that the Lord had shown his great mercy toward

her,
and they rejoiced with her.
When they came on the eighth day to circumcise the child,
they were going to call him Zechariah after his father,
but his mother said in reply,
"No. He will be called John."
But they answered her,
"There is no one among your relatives who has this name."
So they made signs, asking his father what he wished him to be called.
He asked for a tablet and wrote, "John is his name,"
and all were amazed.
Immediately his mouth was opened, his tongue freed,
and he spoke blessing God.
Then fear came upon all their neighbors,
and all these matters were discussed
throughout the hill country of Judea.
All who heard these things took them to heart, saying,
"What, then, will this child be?
For surely the hand of the Lord was with him."

"Immediately his mouth was opened, his tongued freed, and he spoke blessing God." Lk 1:64

Growing up I was the shy type. I cherished my time to myself and never really wanted much to do with others. I was a dreamer, but was never good with following up with those dreams. Because of this I graduated from high school in the bottom point zero one-percentile of my class. When I made my Cursillo weekend I learned how to come out of my shell. I got over my shyness and become more vocal and began giving talks and working with adult education at the parish. Those talks gave way to my true gift, which is writing, and through that God has blessed me richly, loosened my tongue and made me into something more than I could possibly imagine.

We each have a special gift. That gift is unique because God did not make two people the same. Some of us can write, some can speak, some can provide counsel, and some can build. God brings us all together, each with our gifts, to make up one community. Denominations are not what matters here. Race is not important. The things we are measured by are faith and the use of our gifts. The first gift we share is the ability and desire to praise God's name to the ends of the earth. As a community we can no longer be silent. With tongues loosened, mouths opened, our praises lifted, we lay down our gifts at the feet of the child king. And now my life song sings.

4th Tuesday of Advent

1st Reading 2nd Sm 7:1-5, 8B-12, 14A, 16
When King David was settled in his palace,
and the LORD had given him rest from his enemies on every side,
he said to Nathan the prophet,
"Here I am living in a house of cedar,
while the ark of God dwells in a tent!"
Nathan answered the king,
"Go, do whatever you have in mind,
for the LORD is with you."
But that night the LORD spoke to Nathan and said:
"Go, tell my servant David, 'Thus says the LORD:
Should you build me a house to dwell in?

"'It was I who took you from the pasture
and from the care of the flock
to be commander of my people Israel.
I have been with you wherever you went,
and I have destroyed all your enemies before you.
And I will make you famous like the great ones of the earth.
I will fix a place for my people Israel;
I will plant them so that they may dwell in their place
without further disturbance.
Neither shall the wicked continue to afflict them as they did of old,
since the time I first appointed judges over my

people Israel.
I will give you rest from all your enemies.
The LORD also reveals to you
that he will establish a house for you.
And when your time comes and you rest with your ancestors,
I will raise up your heir after you, sprung from your loins,
and I will make his Kingdom firm.
I will be a father to him,
and he shall be a son to me.
Your house and your Kingdom shall endure forever before me;
your throne shall stand firm forever.'"

Psalm Ps 89:2-3, 27 and 29
R. **For ever I will sing the goodness of the Lord.**

The favors of the LORD I will sing forever;
through all generations my mouth shall proclaim your faithfulness.
For you have said, "My kindness is established forever";
in heaven you have confirmed your faithfulness.
R. **For ever I will sing the goodness of the Lord.**

"I have made a covenant with my chosen one,
I have sworn to David my servant:
Forever will I confirm your posterity
and establish your throne for all generations."

R. **For ever I will sing the goodness of the Lord.**

"He shall say of me, 'You are my father,
my God, the rock, my savior.'
Forever I will maintain my kindness toward him,
and my covenant with him stands firm."
R. **For ever I will sing the goodness of the Lord.**

Gospel Lk 1:67-79
Zechariah his father, filled with the Holy Spirit, prophesied, saying:

"Blessed be the Lord, the God of Israel;
for he has come to his people and set them free.
He has raised up for us a mighty Savior,
born of the house of his servant David.
Through his prophets he promised of old
that he would save us from our enemies,
from the hands of all who hate us.
He promised to show mercy to our fathers
and to remember his holy covenant.
This was the oath he swore to our father Abraham:
to set us free from the hand of our enemies,
free to worship him without fear,
holy and righteous in his sight
all the days of our life.
You, my child, shall be called the prophet of the Most High,
for you will go before the Lord to prepare his

way,
to give his people knowledge of salvation
by the forgiveness of their sins.
In the tender compassion of our God
the dawn from on high shall break upon us,
to shine on those who dwell in darkness and the shadow of death,
and to guide our feet into the way of peace."

"The day break from on high will visit us to shine of those who sit in darkness and at deaths shadow." Lk 1:78-79

When I was born I was diagnosed with polycystic kidney disease. Because of this it caused me to wet the bed for 27 years. It was something that made me feel less than whole because I thought that no one else had such a problem. It was difficult for me to love myself or to find anything that was good inside of me. One night several people caught on and removed the costume that I used to mask my insecurities. One of them told me that it takes 28 days to break a habit so I promised myself that I would write something positive about myself each day. Through the love of God in others the daybreak from on high broke upon me and led me from death to life.

There are going to be things in each of our lives that just tear us down. There are things that are going to tell us that we are unlovable and forgotten by God. Sometimes we are going to believe it, but we can overcome each area of darkness in our lives with the light of God's truth and love. The truth is that we are all lovable and deserving of the greatness that God has in mind for each of us. And now my life song sings.

Christmas
Midnight Mass Readings

1st Reading Is 9:1-6
The people who walked in darkness
have seen a great light;
upon those who dwelt in the land of gloom
a light has shone.
You have brought them abundant joy
and great rejoicing,
as they rejoice before you as at the harvest,
as people make merry when dividing spoils.
For the yoke that burdened them,
the pole on their shoulder,
and the rod of their taskmaster
you have smashed, as on the day of Midian.
For every boot that tramped in battle,
every cloak rolled in blood,
will be burned as fuel for flames.
For a child is born to us, a son is given us;
upon his shoulder dominion rests.
They name him Wonder-Counselor, God-Hero,
Father-Forever, Prince of Peace.
His dominion is vast
and forever peaceful,
from David's throne, and over his kingdom,
which he confirms and sustains
by judgment and justice,
both now and forever.
The zeal of the LORD of hosts will do this!

Psalm Ps 96:1-2, 2-3, 11-12, 13
R. **Today is born our Savior, Christ the Lord.**

Sing to the LORD a new song;
sing to the LORD, all you lands.
Sing to the LORD; bless his name.
R. **Today is born our Savior, Christ the Lord.**

Announce his salvation, day after day.
Tell his glory among the nations;
among all peoples, his wondrous deeds.
R. **Today is born our Savior, Christ the Lord.**

Let the heavens be glad and the earth rejoice;
let the sea and what fills it resound;
let the plains be joyful and all that is in them!
Then shall all the trees of the forest exult.
R. **Today is born our Savior, Christ the Lord.**

They shall exult before the LORD, for he comes;
for he comes to rule the earth.
He shall rule the world with justice
and the peoples with his constancy.
R. **Today is born our Savior, Christ the Lord.**

2nd Reading Titus 2:11-14
Beloved:
The grace of God has appeared, saving all
and training us to reject godless ways and worldly desires
and to live temperately, justly, and devoutly in this age,
as we await the blessed hope,
the appearance of the glory of our great God

and savior Jesus Christ,
who gave himself for us to deliver us from all lawlessness
and to cleanse for himself a people as his own,
eager to do what is good.

Gospel Lk 2:1-14
In those days a decree went out from Caesar Augustus
that the whole world should be enrolled.
This was the first enrollment,
when Quirinius was governor of Syria.
So all went to be enrolled, each to his own town.
And Joseph too went up from Galilee from the town of Nazareth
to Judea, to the city of David that is called Bethlehem,
because he was of the house and family of David,
to be enrolled with Mary, his betrothed, who was with child.
While they were there,
the time came for her to have her child,
and she gave birth to her firstborn son.
She wrapped him in swaddling clothes and laid him in a manger,
because there was no room for them in the inn.

Now there were shepherds in that region living in the fields
and keeping the night watch over their flock.
The angel of the Lord appeared to them
and the glory of the Lord shone around them,

and they were struck with great fear.
The angel said to them,
"Do not be afraid;
for behold, I proclaim to you good news of great joy
that will be for all the people.
For today in the city of David
a savior has been born for you who is Christ and Lord.
And this will be a sign for you:
you will find an infant wrapped in swaddling clothes
and lying in a manger."
And suddenly there was a multitude of the heavenly host with the angel,
praising God and saying:
"Glory to God in the highest
and on earth peace to those on whom his favor rests."

"Do not be afraid for behold, I proclaim to you good tidings of great joy that will be for all people. For today in the city of David, a savior has been born for you who is Christ the Lord." Lk 2:10-11

Do you remember the first time you ever kissed your wife or husband? In the moments leading up to the kiss, was there anticipation, fear of the unknown, or just a moment of wanting and waiting? Then it happened – that first moment of sweet connection.

Today marks the day when God become human and connected with us. Christmas takes the love story between God and humanity to a whole new level. For on this day, a savior is born to us. God has come and kissed his people on earth. His love is made visible; we are forgiven, healed, restored, and kissed. Amen. Alleluia! And now my life song sings.

Made in the USA
San Bernardino, CA
13 November 2013